UP THE ROAD

John Harding

Current Theatre Series
Currency Press • Sydney
in association with
Playbox Theatre Centre, Monash University Melbourne

CURRENT THEATRE SERIES

First published in 1997 by
Currency Press Pty Ltd,
PO Box 452 Paddington
NSW 2021, Australia
in association with
Playbox Theatre Centre.

National Library of Australia
Cataloguing-in-Publication data:

Harding, John William 1961–
Up the road

ISBN 0 86819 508 1.

I. Playbox Theatre (Melbourne, Vic.).
II. Title. (Series: Current theatre series).

A822.3

Publication of this title was assisted
by the Commonwealth Government
through the Australia Council, its arts
funding and advisory body.

Set by Currency, Paddington.
Printed by Bridge Printery.

Contents

Contents

Up the Road was first produced by the Ilbijerri Aboriginal and Torres Strait Islander Theatre Co-operative in Melbourne in 1991 with the following cast:

LIDDY	Antoinette Braybrook
AUNT SISSY	Carole Fraser
IAN SAMPSON	Grant Hansen
SUSAN LOCKERBEE	Denice Kickett
GREG HIDCOMBE	Rodney Sharp
RENSHIE / CHARLIE CARDIFF	Glen Shea

Director, Kylie Belling
Designer, Joe Hurst
Production Manager, Maryanne Sam

CHARACTERS

IAN SAMPSON, an outwardly confident, but insecure man aged 30.

AUNT SISSY (often referred to as AUNTIE), matriachal figure, assertive, but with a good sense of humour. She brought Ian up after the death of his parents.

SUSAN LOCKERBEE (often referred to as SUE), quietly spoken, with an inner strength and rationality. An inner hurt has developed her personality. She is 27 years old.

LIDDY, hyperactive day dreamer, incessant chatterer, attractive, about 19 years old. Very forward and cheeky.

CHARLIE CARDIFF, an ambitious dreamer, with a dislike for the prevailing attitudes on the mission. He is a loner through choice, and has a streak of ignorant selfishness. He is 21 years old.

GREG HIDCOMBE, unintentionally patronising white advisor. He is about 40 years old and gets on well with most of the community.

ACT ONE

SCENE ONE

SISSY, SUE *and* LIDDY *are sitting in the lounge of* SISSY'*s house.* SISSY *is very upset and crying.* SUSAN *is comforting her and lightly wiping away her own tears.* LIDDY *and* SISSY *embrace.* SISSY *sits.*

SISSY: When you been with a man as long as I was with Kenny, you never really lose 'em.

SUE: Yeah, Aunt.

SISSY: At least he was with his mate when it happened. At least he wasn't alone. Someone was there. [*She breaks down.*]

SUE: He was one of those people that you think's gonna live forever, wasn't he?

LIDDY: Yeah, I always thought he'd be out there somewhere, shearing or picking apples. Dropping in to see me play a game maybe.

SISSY: And swearing like a trooper at the umpires.

SUE: He would have died happy, Aunt. At least he was doing what he loved.

SISSY: Yeah. Not many people get a kick out of crutching sheep, eh.

SUSAN: He's gonna be missed by so many people. Seems like he spent a week in everyone's life.

LIDDY: He must have been proud of the mission but. How much it's changed.

SISSY: Yeah. He had a lot of plans for this place. Market garden, orchards, and that bloody trout farm. He wanted the boys to learn all the things he'd learnt.

SUSAN: Yeah. That would have been good.

SISSY: But they were never interested really. Ian and Nat weren't anyway.

SUSAN: Nuh.

SISSY: Poor Ian. He's lost them all now. He's the only blood left. I'll call him tomorrow in Canberra.

LIDDY: Ian. Ian Sampson's coming home. Great, eh Sue?

SUSAN: He hasn't been back in ten years. He's not gonna come back now.

SISSY: I'll tell him he's got to come home. He will.

LIDDY: I wonder if he's gone and got married up yet?

SUE: You want to get Aunt a cup of tea, babe?

LIDDY: Alright.

SISSY: Make it a Nescafe, darlin'. I've got tea coming out of my ears.

LIDDY: Okey dokey.

    [LIDDY *exits.*]

SISSY: Ian, eh. You're gunna have to forgive and forget girlie. I remember the day I had to tell them boys about their mum and dad, the car accident. I took them out to that big rock in the gully and sat them on the ground. They were just little boys, Nat and Ian, six or seven. They didn't even cry. Just stared up at me with their big eyes. Like they were sad for me!

SUE: It must have been hard.

SISSY: I couldn't have kids of my own. But I came back from the creek with two sons. Kenny was so proud to take them under his wing.

SUE: Yeah. He loved those boys.

SISSY: Kenny'll be buried right next to Nat. The two wanderers.

    [LIDDY *comes back with a cup of coffee.*]

LIDDY: There you go, Aunt.

SISSY: Thanks love. Forty-three cents in every cup. Who's bringing my Kenny back?

SUE: Pastor Clivey. Billy and Charlie have gone with him.

SISSY: I need to lie down girls. I need to lie down now.

    [SISSY *exits.*]

LIDDY: I'll cook dinner, Aunt. You have a good rest.

SUE: There's a lot of people that have to be rung. He knew bloody everyone.

LIDDY: I'll help with the calls if you like.

SUE: It's OK.

LIDDY: You do A–K and I'll do L–Z. We can use Greg's phones. Ian's an S for Sampson. I'll call him.

SUE: No you won't. Leave it for Aunt Sissy. It's none of your business.

[GREG enters.]

LIDDY: Alright, I'm just trying to help.

GREG: I'm really sorry, guys.

SUE: Hi, Greg.

GREG: I just got back. They told me at the office.

LIDDY: Cuppa tea?

GREG: No, I'm right. How's Aunt Sissy?

SUE: Upset, but she's gone to have a lay down. Pastor Clivey's bringing the body back.

GREG: Well I guess we'll have a lot of phone calls to make, a lot of organising to be done. We'll have to get some mattresses, and extra blankets and sheets. Pillows…

SUE: We better work out a date for the funeral first.

GREG: Of course. How about next Tuesday after the long weekend?

LIDDY: Don't forget the semi finals on Monday!

SUE: That's OK.

GREG: That would give everyone time to arrive and give us time to arrange the service. Lucky it's pension week. People should be right for petrol money and bus fares.

SUE: Thank God you're here, Greg. It's great to have someone I can rely on.

GREG: That's what you pay me for.

SUE: Poor old Kenny, eh? Come here.

[GREG gives SUE a hug.]

GREG: I'm really sorry.

SUE: She's going to need a lot of support, Greg. She loved that man blind in spite of everything.

GREG: I never really got the chance to know Kenny. I offered him a job once when I first started here. He almost seemed angry about it. Grabbed his swag and walked into town.

SUE: Well you know, a man's pride and all. Blackfellas always had more pride than sense.

GREG: Let's not forget the women.

3

SUE: Kenny really got this mob going round here. Made them fight for what they took for granted. They thought no one was gonna disturb them. Kenny kicked them into reality.

GREG: I remember reading about Kenny and that rally you had out here when they were going to develop the golf course and found all those bones.

SUE: Kenny organised that. Mad bugger chained himself to a bobcat with his right arm, and the other to a grader. He even chained his dog to him.

LIDDY: It'd bite the head off anything that come near it.

SUE: We all ended up chained to something or other.

LIDDY: Stupid police even tried to lock me up but I was under age.

GREG: Yeah. I saw it on the telly. That's how I found out this place existed. I must have seen you too. Anyway they shifted the golf course.

SUE: And it helped get us a Land Council.

GREG: Well, I'm grateful for that.

SUE: Blackfella's pride, eh.

GREG: Sure. It's funny, the golf tournament's on next week. There's some Koori irony.

SUE: Imagine if they hadn't moved the golf course.

LIDDY: Uncle Kenny could've been buried on the eighteenth fairway. Scare the shit out of them golfers if a black hand came out of the hole, eh.

    [LIDDY *exits.*]

SUE: I saw a mopoke this morning. It just sat on top of the back shed, watching the house, letting us know.

GREG: They always know, those mopokes.

SCENE TWO

Flat Creek Community Administration Office. A Koori in his early twenties comes bursting through the office door. It's CHARLIE CARDIFF.

CHARLIE: Hey Greg, where are you mate? Greggie. Greggie? You here? Greg? Absent without leave, eh? [*Sits in* GREG's *chair.*] He sure gets a lot of mail for a lad that does fuck all. Advisor! He couldn't advise me how to shit straight. I could do a better job than this arsehole in my sleep. Wouldn't waste my energies on this mob, though. Flat Creek.

[*Music starts.*]
Oh oh. Looks like I have to sing. If that's what you call it. It's not my idea.

SONG: "CHARLIE'S MOAN"

Flat Creek, Flat Creek, even saying it makes me yawn,
Flat Creek, just off shit creek, no wonder I'm forlorn.

If I went to school where they wear a little cap,
I could have been a foreign diplomat,
but Two Rivers High School was never gonna get me there.

Hard dirt tracks and secret fishing spots,
Holes in the road, it's one big parking lot,
but they all think it's the crossroads of the world.

Flat Creek, Flat Creek, even saying it makes me yawn,
Flat Creek, just off shit creek, no wonder I'm forlorn.

We got a whitefella looking after us,
cause as you know you can never really trust a cuz,
If I had a car I'd drive it to the nearest star.
If I had a car.

Rumours and gossip, crowded Koori homes,
I love my fishing so I can be alone,
and dream of leading my crazy mob one day.

What am I saying! No way!
I'd rather drive a car to the nearest star.
If I had a car.

[*Music ends.*]
You can clap now. Ah, look here, hey, he's going for a job with the Australian Institute of Aboriginal and Torres Strait Islander Studies.

[*Starts reading the letter out loud.*]

"As Community Advisor of Flat Creek I have been an integral part of the decision making process and the development of the resources that are now at these people's disposal. Since I began in 1992, we have attained a sports oval", gee thanks Greg, "a basketball court, a new community centre, and tapped several community members into apprenticeships." You're a shoo in. "I am accepted here as a member of the Flat Creek community," [*Mutters to himself*] not by fucken me he's not, "and would be leaving a community which is now well on the way to self determination. Yours faithfully, Gregory L. Hidcombe".

> [GREG *enters.*]

GREG: What are you doing, Charlie?

CHARLIE: Oh, gidday, Greggie, hey I'm surprised to see you up and around with it being Sunday and all.

GREG: What do you mean?

CHARLIE: Well I thought on the seventh day you rested like it says in that book they wrote about you. [*He looks out door.*] So this is heaven, eh? I didn't think there'd be so many blackfellas up here.

> [GREG *laughs.*]

You strong enough for a bite?

GREG: What?

CHARLIE: Well, Gregory, I was just wondering if you could see your way clear to advancing me a small amount till I get my cheque. I will gladly pay you on Tuesday... [*... for a hamburger today.*]

GREG: You spent your dole already?

CHARLIE: Well if I'm gonna have relations staying over next week I want to able to feed them and give them a beer. Especially if my cousin Rick lands on me. He'll eat me out of house and home.

GREG: How's fifty sound?

CHARLIE: That'll do.

GREG: That's all I can afford.

CHARLIE: That'll do. I didn't know it was your money.

GREG: I meant that's all the discretionary fund can afford. We'll have to start your own file soon, Charlie. I'll need your autograph there. Of course if you had a job you wouldn't have to bite me for money.

CHARLIE: Well you always gotta keep your eye out for opportunities, eh?

GREG: Well, if you got your act together… I mean you got through high school. The world's your oyster.

CHARLIE: That's a shame. I don't eat oysters.

GREG: You know what I mean, Charlie.

CHARLIE: Speaking of jobs, how long have you been here, Greg?

GREG: Four years.

CHARLIE: Ever trained anyone to do your job, Greg? No, you just hang around taking credit for everything, like the Land Council's done nothing, then springboard off our backs into the world of white experts.

GREG: I don't think you can honestly say that, Charlie.

CHARLIE: I don't see why not.

GREG: Anyway, I notice you're making great contributions to the community. We can never have enough mullet.

CHARLIE: Hope you don't lose your sense of humour in Canberra. You'll need it.

GREG: Look, I'm not going to Canberra.

CHARLIE: My mistake. God moves in mysterious ways.

GREG: It's just talk. I don't even know if I'd want that job even if I got it.

CHARLIE: Course not, Greg. Why would you want to leave Heaven for? By the way, Greg, what's the "L" stand for?

GREG: Lawrence.

CHARLIE: Really? I thought it was Loverboy…

[*Sings on his way out*] Take the L out of Love and it's over.

> [GREG *puts the cash box away.* IAN *enters. He is dressed in a suit, and has an extra suit in cover and suitcase.*]

IAN: Excuse me. I'm looking for Sissy Cavanagh's house. I'm here for Kenny Cavanagh's funeral.

GREG: Have you just come down from Canberra?

IAN: Yeah but…

GREG: I thought they were going to send the head of the Department. This is a very important funeral you know. What level are you? If you don't mind me asking.

IAN: What fucking level are you?

GREG: Excuse me. I live here! Who are you?

IAN: Who the fuck are you?

> [IAN *grabs* GREG *by the throat.*]

I'm Ian Sampson, Kenny Cavanagh's nephew.

[AUNT SISSY *enters.*]

Auntie!

SISSY: Well, I can see you haven't forgotten the Flat Creek handshake.

IAN: Auntie! How are you?

[*He lets go of* GREG *and hugs his* AUNTIE.]

GREG: Sorry, Auntie Sissy, I didn't know who he was. I thought he was some token jacky sent down from Canberra for the funeral.

SISSY: Hey hey, this jacky can stop our funding tomorrow if he wanted to. So just mind your P's and Q's, Greg.

IAN: It's alright, I shouldn't have lost my head like that. Sorry, Auntie.

GREG: I'm really sorry. Ian. [*Shakes* IAN*'s hand*] Greg Hidcombe, Community Advisor.

IAN: Yeah, I know.

GREG: It's just, well, I've never seen you in the all the time I've been here.

SISSY: Just shut up now, Greg. True, you're about as much assistance round here as a red rag to a bull!!!

IAN: Hey I'm really sorry, Auntie.

SISSY: Don't be. Your Uncle Kenny would've pinned his ears to the desk with his letter opener.

[SUSAN *appears in doorway.*]

SUSAN: At least you've got a bit of fire left, Ian Sampson. I could hear you from the other side of the road.

IAN: [*recognition slowly dawns on* IAN*'s face*] Susie.

SISSY: Come out here Greg. I need to have a yarn with you.

[AUNTIE *and* GREG *go offstage.*]

IAN: How are you?

SUSAN: I've seen better days. What about you? I hear you're climbing the ladder in Canberra.

IAN: I'm doing alright. Shit... it's good to see you again. You haven't changed a bit.

SUSAN: You have. [*She looks him up and down.*] I'm glad you're finally out of those Stubbies.

IAN: Well my legs aren't what they used to be.

SUSAN: Anyway, it didn't have to be nine years.

IAN: For me it did. Look, where I live, I'm something. I've got a great job, I'm well off, own my own house…

SUSAN: Hey, you don't have to prove nothing to me, you stopped having to do that when you left. I don't wanna know why you never came back, OK?

IAN: Yeah, OK.

[Pause.]

Aunt Sissy's looking well.

SUE: Compared to nine years ago. Yeah, I suppose.

IAN: I sort of lost my bearings when I got out of the taxi.

SUE: Forgot where you were for a second?

IAN: All these new houses, office complexes.

SUE: It's just an office, Ian.

IAN: Well, now I'm here, can I do anything to help, Susie?

SUE: How about land rights? Can you order them from Canberra? Nah, everything's organised. Greg and I have got everything under control.

IAN: I suppose there'll be a mob coming across. I hope Auntie saved me a room.

SUSAN: She's been saving it for a long while now.

IAN: I just meant that…

SUE: Yeah, I know what you meant.

IAN: One thing I could do is to have a talk with Greg about future program funding that you guys are eligible to apply for. You can get in early.

SUSAN: The cake's getting smaller, is it Ian?

IAN: It sure is.

SUSAN: Did you ever get homesick?

IAN: It's not like I forgot about everything, I just made a decision to do something with myself.

SUSAN: Uh huh.

IAN: If I remember right, you encouraged me to go.

SUSAN: Yeah, but I didn't encourage you to die!!!

IAN: I didn't die, Susan.

SUSAN: You remember when those lads from DAA would come to the mission and talk to our mob like we were children, and you used to laugh at 'em, and say if you ever went to Canberra you'd kick their doors down and grab 'em by the throat?

9

IAN: That was before I understood.

SUSAN: No, that's when you understood perfectly.

[GREG *enters*.]

GREG: Excuse me, I just need to grab my car keys.

SUE: Where are you off to, Greg?

GREG: Got to go into town, get some supplies. The mob's arriving.

SUE: I've got to do some shopping too. I'll grab Lutana and come with you.

[SUSAN *exits*.]

GREG: Sure, you know I'd drive you anywhere... Sweetie! Is there anything we can get you while we're in there, Ian?

IAN: Could you grab me some beers? Uh, light beers. I forgot how hot it is out here. Hey Greg, who's Lutana?

GREG: The daughter of course.

IAN: Of course.

SCENE THREE

AUNTIE SISSY's *loungeroom. It's raining outside.* IAN *is sitting writing in his journal.* LIDDY *appears, looks around and smiles to herself.*

LIDDY: It's good, isn't it?

IAN: Yeah, it is... sorry, what?

LIDDY: It's good that I can talk to a fella that's not my cousin, I mean, you know what I mean. I mean we're not blood relations. That's my problem you know. Koories take relating so laterally.

IAN: You mean literally.

LIDDY: You too?! That's what I mean: why it's good to talk to a fella with a bit of edumacation... na, only gammin'. [*She giggles.*]

IAN: What do you do, Liddy, I mean you don't go to school anymore do you?

LIDDY: Na, I could've taught the teachers when I was in Year Seven. They thought I was stupid. Trouble is I don't think the way they do. They didn't realize I was answering their questions

10

before they asked 'em, you know to save them the trouble, like. What are you writing?

IAN: Just work.

LIDDY: Oh you don't, you do, you keep a diary.

IAN: It's not a diary, it's a filofax.

LIDDY: What's that?

IAN: Just a flash diary.

LIDDY: Oh, can I have a read of September 5th? That's my birthday.

IAN: I'll read it out to you. "9.30 am: edumacation meeting, Lower Plaza; 11.30 am: ring mechanic; 12pm: Truscott lawyers re Katherine project; 1pm: lunch Department Head.

LIDDY: Did you leave the eyes in so he could see the bill?

IAN: What?

LIDDY: Only gammin'. Go on please.

IAN: 2:00 pm: staff meeting; 3 pm: accountants re Trust settlement.

LIDDY: You did all that on my birthday? I spent all day in the pub. I was drinkin' Tequila Sunrises and eating Oyster Kilpatricks. I was sick as a dog. Probably while you was at the Trust Settlement.

IAN: [*laughing*] Well on my birthday I was blind in Woden.

LIDDY: Aunt Sissy says they're all blind in Woden. Oh, no offence, eh? What's it like in Canberra? Lots of pretty Koorie girls I suppose, an' they're all single too, an' up themselves.

IAN: Yes there are, and no they're not, and no they're not.

LIDDY: What do you do for fun? Do you go out raging? Are there nightclubs in Canberra? Have you got a woman?

IAN: [*laughing*] Yes I do, yes there are, and no I haven't. Oh Liddy, you an' your questions.

LIDDY: Did you think about Susan very much?

IAN: No more questions, OK Liddy.

LIDDY: How could you do it then, Ian?

IAN: Do what?

LIDDY: I mean if you were mad in love with someone up there, I could understand it but to be by yourself and not ring for nearly ten years, I would've been lost.

IAN: It's not easy to get lost in Flat Creek.

LIDDY: I mean it's a long time to be away from your family. All the people who love you.

IAN: I don't want to talk about it, Liddy, OK?

LIDDY: OK. Sorry. It doesn't matter.

IAN: Good.

LIDDY: Hey have I changed much? Last time you saw me I was ten years old.

IAN: Yes, you've grown into a real woman, Liddy.

LIDDY: I'm my own person now. Hey, I might come and stop in Canberra for a while.

> [*She sits.*]

IAN: Oh, yeah well, there's plenty of flats, and uh, I'm sure we could find you something...

LIDDY: No, I mean at your place, I'm a great cook, as long as there's eggs in the fridge. I could probably get a job, must be lots of secretaries' jobs an' that. Will you promise me you'll think about it, I don't wanna rush you, but maybe if you can't live here, you can take a bit of the mish with ya.

IAN: I promise you I'll think about it, Liddy. OK?

> [LIDDY *grabs diary and begins to write in it.*]

LIDDY: Yeah. Well there's not much else to think about. It's raining outside, the tele's broken, and Pastor Clivey's borrowed my tape deck. [*She giggles.*] I like you Ian, you're alright.

IAN: I like you too, Liddy.

LIDDY: The netball team would miss me but. I was best and fairest last year, and shot the winning goal in the Grand Final.

IAN: I wish I could've seen it.

LIDDY: You could have, you could've been *right* there.

> [*Pause.* LIDDY *gets up and moves to the door. She suddenly remembers to give him his diary back.*]

See ya then!

IAN: See ya then! [*Sees what she's written and smiles to himself.*] 14th February. Don't forget to send a big bunch of roses and a box of Cadburys for your darling Valentine, Susan Lockerbee.

SCENE FOUR

AUNTIE SISSY *is sitting on the edge of her bed. She is talking to Uncle Kenny.*

SISSY: I know you can hear me, darlin', you could always hear me. Couldn't ya. You're just a little bit further away, but I can still see you. I can still smell ya. You can still see me too can't ya, darlin'. All the families are here for you now. Margaret and Teddy have come up with their two boys. The Thurrill mob came all the way down. You used to always blue with them, but they loved ya. Lois and Kevin brought all their kids up to say goodbye. Remember little Kenny, your namesake. He's still got asthma though, eh. A lot of your shearing mates are coming, and a couple of your old bosses. I know you know Ian's here. You said he'd come, and it was you that brought him. He's a good lad, just confused and lonely, that's all. Just confused and lonely.
  [SUSAN *enters.*]
SUE: Do you want a cup of tea, Aunt?
SISSY: Yeah thanks, babe.
SUE: Here ya go. I already made you one.
SISSY: Never say no to a cuppa. Thanks, babe.
SUSAN: I was wondering where everyone is. Charlie was round. Took Ian down the pub to play the pokies. He's gonna help him blow his travel allowance.
SISSY: Yeah, that'd be Charlie Cardiff.
SUSAN: How are you feeling, Auntie?
SISSY: Old and tired, as usual. But a bit better than I was yesterday. Why don't you go and join them, get away from us girls for a while. It'd give you a chance to talk.
SUE: Yeah, it'd be a real intimate cosy chat. Me, Ian and the poker machine. No, it's alright Aunt. I think we've run our race. He's done fine without me all these years. I don't think he needs some mission gin messing up his life.

SISSY: Oh stop talking like that. If it wasn't for us women they'd all be running around like lost souls. Some of them still are.

SUE: Sometimes you just got to be content with what you got.

SISSY: You sound like an old woman sometimes, true. Since when were you brought up to settle for second best, eh? Is that what you tell your girls every Wednesday night?

SUE: No.

SISSY: No. Course not. You gotta go for gold, darlin'.

SUSAN: Oh Auntie, if only life was as simple as a netball game, eh.

SISSY: Life's what you make it. You gotta look out for number one, eh.

SUSAN: I haven't got time to worry about myself, not with the mission taking up every spare minute of the day.

SISSY: Well you got a daughter to worry about too. Without the kids out there, there's no point worrying about the mission. I reckon Lutana needs a father.

SUE: Oh yeah. Where's she gonna find one?

SISSY: I reckon Ian's got that dewy look in his eyes…

SUSAN: What Lutana needs is someone who's loving, reliable and most of all, there for her. So that rules out Ian Sampson on all three counts.

SISSY: Oh well, the way I look at it, you got two choices…

SUSAN: Auntie, can we change the subject please?

SISSY: I just want you to be happy girl, that's all.

SUSAN: Yeah. I spoke to Greg earlier, and it sounds like everything's under control. He's got Pastor Clivey helping out too.

SISSY: Did I ever tell you that Clivey became a pastor right after I married Kenny? He said if he couldn't have me, then God was the next best thing.

SUE: You must have been a real looker.

SISSY: [patting her hair] Ohhh, nooo!

SUE: Why don't you lie down for a while now and I'll wake you when Tattslotto's on alright?

SISSY: Yeah, got to be in it to win it.

[SUSAN exits.]

Buy a big tombstone then, eh darlin?

GREG *and* LIDDY *are out the back porch of* AUNTIE SISSY'*s house.*
LIDDY *is preparing for her anticipated triumph on the netball court.*

GREG: I hope you like the leg of lamb. Butcher said it should be quite tender. Maybe you could cook Ian a feed of it.

LIDDY: I can't. I'm having dinner with Tom Cruise.

GREG: He seems like a smart bloke, Ian. Must be to get that high up in Canberra at his age.

LIDDY: He was always smart, even as a kid. He even stayed at school till year eleven you know.

GREG: What was he like as a kid? Cheeky I bet.

LIDDY: He had a wild head of hair, long skinny legs dangling down from his Stubbie shorts and he always smelt like the Creek. He's still got beautiful eyes though, eh.

GREG: I wouldn't know.

LIDDY: Oh yeah. And he never took crap from no one.

GREG: He and Susan… they known each other long?

LIDDY: Since they was kids. Aunt Sissy reckons he started chasing Susan around from the time she learned to run away. They were mad sweet on each other, did you know that? Susan would have told you that.

GREG: Oh yeah, I think Susan did mention something about a childhood sweetheart but we didn't go into details.

LIDDY: I was only little then, they used to take me riding on the back of the horse with them. They used to go skinny dipping in Flat Creek. It wasn't flat when they hit the water though, eh.

GREG: That was a long time ago, eh, I mean if he really liked someone he wouldn't just disappear on her would he? Anyway, she certainly seems to be over him now.

LIDDY: [*noncommittal*] Oh yeah.

GREG: Well, she hasn't spoken to me about him in the whole four years I've been here.

LIDDY: When I was at school, the biology teacher told us about the praying mantis. The man one goes to the woman when she calls him even though he knows after they do the damage, have sex, she is going to kill him and eat him. That's the most romantic story I ever heard. Now that's Lerv. Wish I could find a man like that.

GREG: He, Ian, I mean, well, do you think he still fancies Susan?

LIDDY: I haven't seen him for nearly ten years. He could be gay for all I know.

GREG: Do you think so?

LIDDY: Well Canberra does funny things to people.

GREG: I wonder how he'd feel about little Lutana though. Black men don't like fathering other men's children, at least that's what I've heard.

LIDDY: And all white men have got pippies like this [*Holds up her little finger.*] at least that's what I've heard. But you can't believe everything you hear, eh?

GREG: No, I suppose not. I mean in relation to what I'm talking about.

LIDDY: I used to do the canteen at the Flat Creek Rovers footy club, right next to the changing rooms, and believe me you can't believe everything you hear. [*Laughs.*]

GREG: I don't think Susan would handle living in Canberra though. She's been here for too long.

LIDDY: We've all been here too long. That's why I reckon it's hard to move into tomorrow for us mob. We're still working out how to take yesterday with us. Maybe Ian forgot that for a while.

GREG: Do you think he's a bit of a "coconut", black on the outside, white on the inside? He seems a bit flash.

LIDDY: He's just trying to beat the whitefellas at their own game, that's all. He's smart enough as well. Naa, I think he looks spunky in his raw silk suit. Looks real fine! I bet Susan does too. Underneath.

GREG: He's a Senior Officer Class C, so with that kind of money, he could certainly provide for the two of them.

LIDDY: Geez, I might have to get him to adopt me too, eh, or you could. What are we paying you?

GREG: $30,000.

LIDDY: I thought it was more than that.

GREG: I'm not here for the money. If that was all I was interested in, I'd be in Canberra.

LIDDY: Won't you be?

GREG: What?

LIDDY: I mean eventually.

GREG: Well, maybe.

LIDDY: Maybe.

GREG: One day.

LIDDY: One day.

GREG: There's a lot of jobs going there. And security.

LIDDY: Only security we got here is social, eh?

GREG: At least you people got each other. And the land grant.

LIDDY: Uncle Kenny used to say when whitefellas came we had the land and they had the Bible. Now we got the Bible and they've got the land. But we got a bit of ours back, eh.

GREG: You know, it's a funny thing but I almost feel guilty about being white sometimes. I know I shouldn't but, well there are times I feel I don't quite fit in. To tell you the truth, I think Susie and I could be better friends if I had happened to have been born a blackfella.

LIDDY: But just because you got something in common with someone, it doesn't always mean you'll like them more. Even tigers attack each other unna?

GREG: Yeah, that's true. I mean, for instance, I think Aunt Sissy and I have a good understanding, despite our cultural differences. We're very much on the same wave length. I'm even starting to finish her sentences for her.

LIDDY: Well pretty soon you'll be starting to start her sentences for her too.

GREG: Well it helps me with my work to be able to pre-empt what Aunt Sissy would say when I'm in meetings with those bureaucrats.

LIDDY: Yeah, I bet it does.

GREG: You know I haven't told many people this but once I went on a spirituality camp.

LIDDY: A what?

17

GREG: The intention was that we get more in touch with ourselves and you know, in tune with our auras. An inner journey begins with a single thought.

LIDDY: Well that's true.

GREG: Funny thing was, as I was focussing after we'd meditated for a while, I kept seeing this black man in my mind's eye.

LIDDY: True. What a spinout.

GREG: Yeah. He was speaking in a language I didn't know.

LIDDY: Go on please.

GREG: But I understood every word of it. I even spoke back to him.

LIDDY: Get out of town!

GREG: The Koori fella who was running the workshop told me that we were symbolically communicating across time. And across the cosmos itself.

LIDDY: Great.

GREG: Yeah.

[GREG and LIDDY *stare up at the night sky.*]

LIDDY: It's a funny old world.

SCENE SIX

IAN *and* CHARLIE *sit in a bar surrounded by poker machines.*

IAN: I always have a dash of lime in my beer. Takes the tang out. Makes for easier drinking.

CHARLIE: Sounds a bit poofie to me. You can order them for me next time—Shame job. And a fucking midi, of light!

IAN: I'm on my best behaviour.

CHARLIE: That's not what I hear. You know Aunt Sissy's cousin's stepfather's ex-girlfriend was working as a temp in Canberra and she saw you in a tavern. She said you were pissed as, and looked like you had a drinking problem

IAN: I got no problem brother. I get drunk, I fall down, go to sleep, wake up, go home! No problem!

CHARLIE: Yeah, well that's not what they reckon up here. You know what the Koori grapevine's like, cuz.

IAN: Canberra's funny like that. No blackfellas want to work there, but everyone's got a relation that does.

CHARLIE: Naa.

IAN: I could blame a lot of things on why I drink. A lot of people say they do it to forget. Me, I do it to remember.

CHARLIE: Remember what?

IAN: I dunno. I been sober that long I forgot.

CHARLIE: Aw…

IAN: When I was on the plane flying in, I looked down and saw all the houses laid out like little boxes and the Creek winding through. I was trying to remember what you would all look like, how old you would all be now. I felt like I didn't want to get off the plane. I feel funny about being here. People look at me like I'm from another planet. Like I've let somebody down or something. Makes me feel all jangly.

CHARLIE: Well I'm afraid your hour's up. That'll be fifty bucks and I'll see you next week. Nah, I know what your saying, cuz. I probably go fishing for the same reasons. Anyways you probably got more money than you know what to do with. How much they pay you Ian, in Canberra, if you don't mind me asking?

IAN: Forty-one thousand dollars a year and all the arse you can lick.
    [*They laugh.*]
    No, it's good. I got it pretty good. Better than most.

CHARLIE: Yeah but for how long? See, this government, this government don't like blackfellas and they don't believe in self determination. I read the papers. Half the blacks are under investigation and the other half's doing the accusing. I wouldn't be surprised if they sunk the lot of us.

IAN: It'll never happen, Charlie. We've come too far now. We've got laws now so it can't be reversed. What with Mabo, Reconciliation Council, Native Title Tribunals…

CHARLIE: All I know is what the white man giveth, the white man can taketh away. Show me a law that says he can't, cuz.

IAN: The High Court of Australia is the highest in the land.

CHARLIE: What about our law?

IAN: What do you think I'm fighting for?

CHARLIE: Good luck.

IAN: I could be going to Geneva next year, if I get selected.

19

CHARLIE: What for? Rugby League?

IAN: No. To the World Conference of Indigenous Peoples. That's where we could really make our voice heard. Hundreds of people go.

CHARLIE: Who selects you to go?

IAN: The Minister for Aboriginal Affairs.

CHARLIE: That's arse up. Seems arse up to me. Don't you think that's arse up?

IAN: Yeah it's arse up.

CHARLIE: You're like generals with no armies.

IAN: Someone's got to be in the front line, Charlie.

CHARLIE: Speakin' of, cuz, how's about we get in the front line of them pokies instead, cuz? Lend me ten, we'll pump in twenty, an' I'll go you halves if we win. I get me cheque next week.

[IAN *gives him ten dollars.*]

IAN: I won't be here next week. Just take it.

CHARLIE: Ta, cuz. I'll get some change for us.

[CHARLIE *begins to exit.*]

IAN: Grab us some beers while you're there.

[CHARLIE *holds out his hand for more cash.* IAN *gives more cash.*]

CHARLIE: Go grab a machine. Try and get that one in the middle there, it's got the Koori colours, might be lucky.

IAN: It's just a paint job. Have you ever won on it?

CHARLIE: Na, but you gotta keep backing the colours, eh? Wouldn't you cry if someone else got the jackpot, and it should have been yours?

IAN: Yeah, I suppose.

[CHARLIE *exits.*]

Hurry up with the midis, eh.

CHARLIE: In Flat Creek, we drink schooners. And whisky chasers.

IAN: Don't forget the dash of lime!!

[*Music.* IAN *sings "Wasted Days and Wasted Nights".*
IAN *and* CHARLIE *are staggering home along the track with a carton of beers.*]

No, you're probably just the right age to be thinking about a career, young man. There's a lot of opportunities in Canberra.

CHARLIE: You haven't been listening bud. The Nazis are marching in Europe and the old Anzac spirit is gonna get its arse kicked.

The well is gonna dry up and all you blackfellas with your deadly cars and mobiles better trade 'em in for a fishing rod and a gun.

IAN: You don't know what the fuck you're talking about. Blackfellas are finally getting senior positions in ATSIC. Look at me. I'm the South-Western Cross-Sectoral Co-ordinating Policy Adviser.

CHARLIE: Don't you talk dirty to me.

IAN: Nah true. I've got huge responsibilities, and this region's one of them.

CHARLIE: You mean to tell me you're one of our regional big shots and we didn't even know. Oh that's a good one.

IAN: A letter would've went to the Land Council when I first got the promotion.

CHARLIE: You mean they sent it to Greg, our resident saint. Here, carry this for a bit. Hey did you know that Bob Hawke's son was working as an adviser in some Aboriginal community? They're fucken mad mate. I would have held him for ransom. "Implement land rights legislation or we flush the bastard." [*Putting trigger finger to* IAN'*s head.*]

IAN: Stop it will you. I'll drop these fuckin' things. Hey, I used to walk this way home with Nat some nights. He used to tell me these ghost stories, and put the wind right up me. One time he threw a rock in the bushes while I wasn't looking. I took off that fast I ran straight into a tree. Nearly killed myself.

CHARLIE: I came off Pope the other day and hit a tree. Did you know that my horse, Pope, is out of Dyson, Uncle Kenny's horse?

IAN: Dyson, she was a beautiful horse. I remember one time when Uncle Kenny was home, he took me riding with him on her. She spotted a rabbit and we followed it so close we were treading on its tail for about four hundred yards. I must have been about eight years old and I was hanging on to Uncle Kenny. Felt like we were flying. Shit, I haven't ridden a horse for years.

CHARLIE: Well, bruz, forget the fifty bucks I owe you, and you can ride Pope whenever you want to.

IAN: Thanks, bruz ! Here have another one, lighten the load, eh?

CHARLIE: Ta, bruz.

IAN: Susie got anyone after her these days, bruz? She got a man on the side or anything?

CHARLIE: No, she's closed her heart. But that Greg's sniffing around all the time. Thinks having a gin will give him some credibility.

IAN: True. The poxy dog.

CHARLIE: Yeah, I reckon the only reason she had the one nighter with that footballer was to have a kid. At least she had a pretty one.

IAN: Who was he? Is he local?

CHARLIE: Nah, he was a long tall streak of black fucken misery named Len Towser. He was with the Melbourne team that came up for the footy knockout.

[IAN *and* CHARLIE *sing.*]

SONG: "THE ALL BLACKS SONG"

We keep the ball in motion, just like a rollin' ocean,
All blacks play the game.
We keep the forwards busy, until their heads get dizzy,
All blacks play the game.
And if the other fella puts a little dirt in, we'll do just the
    same,
We keep the ball in motion, just like a rollin' ocean,
All blacks play the game.

[*They exit, passing the carton from one to the other. A loud crash is heard.*]

CHARLIE: Meeeeedic!!!

SCENE SEVEN

AUNT SISSY'*s loungeroom. Monday of the long weekend.* IAN *sits on the couch asleep, with a beer can still in his hand. He is snoring.* AUNTIE SISSY *appears in the doorway, shaking her head.*

SISSY: [*shaking her head*] Oh, this boy of ours, what are you really drinkin' for I wonder? [*Takes can out of his hand.*] You're home now, my boy. You got no need to drink this no more.

[SUSAN *enters.*]

SUSAN: Mornin', Auntie Sissy.

SISSY: Mornin', darlin'. Could you get this fella's shoes off and push him up on the couch? I'll just get the kettle on. Watch his breath. It'll burn the hair out of your nostrils.

[AUNTIE *leaves the room.*]

SUSAN: Sure, Aunt. Not taking his shoes off but. Big night, eh, big boy...

[SUE *watches* IAN, *then pulls the pillow out from under his head.* LIDDY *enters reading* IAN's *diary.*]

LIDDY: It's a wonder this fella has time to sleep at all. Look at all the meetings he goes to.

SUSAN: Liddy, give me that bloody thing. What do you think you're doing reading his diary?

LIDDY: There's nothing personal in it, except for the weekends. He's mad on some woman named Delilah.

SUSAN: It's none of your business, Liddy, how would you like someone reading your diary? Now get in the kitchen and help Aunt with the tea before I tell her about your nosin' around.

[SUSAN *snatches diary from* LIDDY.]

LIDDY: Awright, awright, geez. Anyway, it's not a diary. It's a filofax.

[LIDDY *goes.* SUSAN *checks doorway, then* IAN, *looks in diary.*]

CHARLIE: Anyone home?

SISSY: [*off*] Who's that?

CHARLIE: Hello.

SUSAN: Come in.

CHARLIE: Oh gidday, I was just gonna see if this fella wanted to do some fishin' this morning.

SUSAN: Good luck.

CHARLIE: I promised him last night I'd show him my secret spot. Hey Ian. Ian. Geez, he looks a bit green about the gills.

SUSAN: Yeah. Wonder why.

CHARLIE: [*laughs*] He knows some fella runs a trawler off Ulladulla. He said he might be able to put a good word in for me.

SUSAN: Oh great, you're the first Koori in the district to get their HSC, and now you're gonna leave us too.

CHARLIE: All the more reason, isn't it?

SUSAN: Seems to me us women bring you men into the world, rear you up, go without for you, then when you're big enough to look after yourself, that's exactly what you do. Then when you're a hero, you expect us women to clap. And if you want a biscuit, put the lid back on the tin!

CHARLIE: Now don't go talkin' them feministic attitudes in Auntie Sissy's house. You know what she thinks of them feminists.

SUSAN: Don't bloody patronise me, Charlie Cardiff. Why don't you go and join your brother here in his ivory tower in Canberra?

CHARLIE: Better than being joined at the hip with Greg fucking skidmark.

SUSAN: Don't you rubbish Greg Hidcombe to me, Charlie Cardiff. He's done more for the people of this community than all you black men put together.

CHARLIE: That's classic. Is that what you said to Uncle Kenny? He founded that Land Council and then you go and bring this whitefella in to run it.

SUSAN: Don't talk about Uncle Kenny with Aunt Sissy in the next room alright, Charlie. You got too much to say.

CHARLIE: Especially when no one wants to listen, that's why I'm out of here.

SUSAN: Yeah, well off you go. That's really going to help your mob.

CHARLIE: And what are you doing to help? What did Pastor Doug say? "Yous let 'em feed us like chooks when we're supposed to be eagles."

SUSAN: Eagles don't leave their nests. Ulladulla fulla. [*Off*] Liddy, where's that bloody tea?

CHARLIE: Women! Can't live with 'em, can't feed 'em to the sharks.
    [SISSY *enters*.]

SISSY: Yeah. I'll give you sharks, Charlie Cardiff. You ought to have more sense. What's the idea of taking Ian down the pub and getting him rotten drunk before the funeral. You ought to have more respect.

CHARLIE: Sorry Auntie. I thought…

SISSY: Thought. You don't think, that's your problem. You just talk big, drink whisky and smoke that stuff.

CHARLIE: But…

SISSY: What do they call it? "Dope", that's right. They don't call it "smart", eh?

CHARLIE: He's only here…

SISSY: And get that damn bucket out of my living room. It stinks to high heaven.

[SISSY *exits.*]

SUSAN: She seems a bit better.

CHARLIE: Ian, we got a creek full of fish waiting for us.

IAN: Geez Charlie, I'm crook as a dog. I don't know if I could look a mullet in the eye this morning brother.

CHARLIE: Well I'm gonna go and pull some up from the mud. I'll bring you back some lunch. Catch yous.

[CHARLIE *exits.*]

SUSAN: That fella, sometimes I think he's covered in Gladwrap. Nothing seems to penetrate him, but I'm sure he can see us.

IAN: I think Charlie's gonna be a good fisherman.

SUSAN: *What* are you talking about?

IAN: I don't know, I'm too crook.

[LIDDY *enters with a cup of coffee and a glass of Berocca.*]

LIDDY: There you are, Mr Sampson, a cup of milky coffee and a Berocca to go.

IAN: Not so loud.

LIDDY: Why don't you come to the netball with us, take your mind off your hangover? There's nothing you can do around here and we'll be back by lunchtime.

IAN: Why not indeed? I probably need to get out in the sun and clear my head. It's not every day I get to see the "Flat Creek Fury" in action.

LIDDY: That's right, cuz.

IAN: Shhh.

[GREG *enters.*]

GREG: Morning everybody.

LIDDY: Morning, Greg.

SUE: Hi, Greg.

GREG: I've got all the gear ready, Suze.

SUSAN: Good.

GREG: I've got some resin for your shoes, a spare tunic. Even got a whistle to confuse the enemy. [*Blows whistle.*] Come on, we'll be leaving in a second.

SUSAN: Thank God there's one man around here that's sober.

GREG: [*to* IAN] You're welcome to come along mate. If you don't mind riding in the back of the ute.

LIDDY: I'll get in the back, Ian. You can sit in the front next to Sue.

SUE: There's not enough room.

IAN: It's OK. I'll walk.

LIDDY: Why don't we all walk?

GREG: Don't be silly. You've got to save your energy for the game. Sue, you OK? Let's go.

LIDDY: See ya, Auntie Sissy.

SISSY: [*off*] Up the Tigers.

[GREG *and* SUE *call goodbye to* SISSY *and exit with* LIDDY.]

IAN: I'll see you there.

SCENE EIGHT

IAN *and* SUSAN *are watching* LIDDY *on the netball court. Whistles and cheers can be heard in the background.* SUSAN *enters and coaches game.*

SUSAN: C'mon, c'mon c'mon. That's it. Share the ball! Good!

[IAN *enters.*]

IAN: Where's your mate?

SUSAN: Who?

IAN: Greg.

SUSAN: He's doing the half time oranges.

IAN: That's nice of him.

SUSAN: Nice play!

IAN: She's pretty good, isn't she?! A real natural.

SUSAN: *I've* trained Liddy since she was ten.

26

PLAYBOX THEATRE CENTRE AND COMPANY B BELVOIR PRESENT

UP THE ROAD

BY JOHN HARDING

CAST

GREG HIDCOMBE	**Paul Blackwell/ Geoff Kelso***
CHARLIE CARDIFF	**Bradley Byquar**
AUNT SISSY	**Lillian Crombie**
SUSAN LOCKERBEE	**Margaret Harvey**
IAN SAMPSON	**John Moore**
LIDDY	**Irma Woods**

PRODUCTION

DIRECTOR	**Neil Armfield**
SET DESIGNER	**Brian Thomson**
COSTUME DESIGNER	**Anna Borghesi**
LIGHTING DESIGNER	**Mark Howett**
ASSISTANT LIGHTING DESIGNER	**Steven Hawker**
MUSIC	**Wayne Freer**
ASSISTANT DIRECTOR AND ASSISTANT STAGE MANAGER	**Jilli Romanis**
DRAMATURG	**Francesca Smith**
PRODUCTION MANAGER	**Andrew Barker/Adam Quinn**
PRODUCTION CO-ORDINATOR	**Brenna Hobson**
STAGE MANAGER	**Tanya Bennett**
TECHNICAL MANAGER	**Stuart McKenzie**
TOUR MANAGER	**David Roberts**
THEATRE TECHNICIAN	**Frank Stoffels**
WARDROBE CO-ORDINATOR	**Jane Hyland**
WARDROBE ASSISTANT	**Sara Tinning**
WORKSHOP SUPERVISOR	**Colin Orchard**
SCENIC ARTIST	**Marie Orchard**
SET CONSTRUCTION	**Playbox Workshop Staff**

* Paul Blackwell appears in Perth and Melbourne seasons and Monash on April 2 and 5. Geoff Kelso appears in Sydney season and Monash on April 1, 3 and 4.
Up the Road was first produced by Ilbijerri Aboriginal and Torres Strait Islander Theatre Co-operative in Melbourne in 1991.
This production of *Up the Road* is dedicated to the memory of Eleanor Harding.

JOHN HARDING
PLAYWRIGHT

Born and raised in Melbourne, John has worked with the Aboriginal community for many years. He has been a ministerial adviser for the Victorian Department of Aboriginal Affairs, Senior Project Officer for the Aboriginal Education Department and National Aboriginal Employment Co-ordinator for the Australian Film Commission. He was Assistant Director for the 1989 National Black Playwrights' Conference, Artistic Director of the 1996 Nambundah Festival and in 1990, a founding member of the Ilbijerri Aboriginal Theatre Co in Melbourne, for which he originally wrote *Up the Road*. It was then presented at the 1995 Australian Playwrights' Conference. Radio credits include *Land Rights, Rally* and *Blackman and Sobbin* and for television an episode of *Lift Off* and *Blackout*. Recent credits for SBS-TV include developing and producing the Aboriginal sitcom *The Masters* and the SBS indigenous current affairs program, *ICAM*.

PLAYWRIGHT'S NOTE

The origins of *Up the Road* came from a visit to Canberra... The Federal Minister for Aboriginal Affairs said to me, "It's better for a person with no responsibilities to work in the department responsible for indigenous people." There was something ironic in this opinion, yet quite well meaning from his point of view. This has been the basis of many of the problems my people face today.

The play's other origin was to challenge the view that we are an homogenous group... When black communities have different opinions we are either: in-fighting or "blacks can't make their minds up". This dehumanises us and makes it easier to ignore the fact that we are a dozen "Europes".

Up the Road is about a family who have been affected by all this... Salvation may be just up the road, but we'll never know until we get there and create it. Doesn't mean we can't have a good laugh getting there.

John Harding

Qantas is
proud to support
Playbox Theatre
Centre of Monash
University

NEIL ARMFIELD
DIRECTOR

Neil Armfield is Artistic Director of Company B, has directed many works for theatre, opera and television over the past 17 years and has given a lot of pleasure.

DIRECTOR'S NOTE

When I first read *Up the Road*, I was struck by its wit, tenderness, the vivid sense of place that inhabits it but above all by the remarkable characters which make up its cast.

The script has been through many transformations. From the original play directed by Kylie Belling in 1991, through the 1995 Australian National Playwrights' Conference where under the direction of Noel Tovey and dramaturgy of Mary-Anne Gifford, the play started to expand. The greatest transformation however has occurred over the past few months and in particular since we started rehearsal. This potentially nerve wracking process has actually been quite pleasurable and for this I must thank John Harding for his willingness to experiment, the cast and all those involved for their good ideas and sense of collaboration; and Nick Enright for his perceptions about structure at a number of critical moments.

The production itself is quite playful – with a sense of very true and deep moments of connection between characters in a larger context of highly self conscious performance. This is not an arch or 'arty' choice but (I hope) touches the play lightly, and helps its communication to be relaxed and quite immediate. We have played with music and song not from the desire to create some kind of Clayton's musical, but because the songs help break open the play's form and allow for a different kind of revelation of character and performance. (If you sense something of the lounge room family concert you are probably not wrong.)

The guiding principle throughout has been common to all the work at Company B; the actors sharing a story with the audience from a corner of space in which we all stand.

Neil Armfield

Culinary and Cultural Oasis... Healthy Homemade food in a wonderful atmosphere....

The Malthouse Café has fresh muffins, bountiful lunch rolls, tasty frittatas, pies and salads, healthy soups and tempting daily specials. And of course, we make sublime coffee and cakes (the tira mi su is truly indulgent!)

Or relax with a beer or wine in our courtyard.

We're open from 8am weekdays and from midday on weekends.

malthouse café

113 sturt street south melbourne 3205 telephone 96 85 51 05

TANYA BENNETT
STAGE MANAGER

For Playbox, Tanya has stage managed *Honour*, *The Incorruptible*, *Burning Time*, *Jerusalem* and *The Mourning After* and was Assistant Stage Manager for *Gary's House* and both seasons of *Emma: Celebrazione!* In 1992, Tanya worked for Zootango Theatre Company in Hobart where her stage managing credits include *Cosi, Barmaids, As You Like It, Comedy of Errors, Alice in Wonderland, Wind in the Willows* and *A Midsummer Night's Dream*. She was also Assistant Stage Manager for the Hobart season of *Money and Friends* for the QTC. Other credits include *Test Tube Twin Set* for the Melbourne Comedy Festival and *Fairy Tales – The Future* for the Melbourne Fringe Festival.

PAUL BLACKWELL
ACTOR

Paul graduated from NIDA in 1981 and since then has worked extensively in theatre. Credits include *The Venetian Twins, A Flea in her Ear, Jonah, Restoration* and *The Comedy of Errors* for the State Theatre of South Australia; *Two Weeks with the Queen, Away, The Government Inspector* and *The Ham Funeral* for the Sydney Theatre Company; *Picasso at the Lapin Agile, Frogs, Popular Mechanicals I* and *II* and *Royal Commission into the Australian Economy* for Company B Belvoir. Television credits include *Patrol Boat II, The Keepers* and *The Seven Deadly Sins* for the ABC; *Clowning Around Encore!* and for SBS, *3 4 Ever.* Film credits include *On Our Selection* and *The Quiet Room* which was included in The Palm d'Or Official Selections at the 1996 Cannes Film Festival.

ANNA BORGHESI
COSTUME DESIGNER

Anna is a designer of small, medium and large sets, costumes, hair dos, hair don'ts, shoes, cats, gardens and the occasional Victorian residence on which she performs a lovely rustic number with a verandah late in the day. Having trained in the fine drafting school of the Kalgoorlie mining industry and NIDA she developed her penchant for the Moorish fan, the Latin ragging and the mottled Mediterranean scallop. Her work thus far has included, for Neil Armfield, *Night on Bald Mountain*, *Angels in America Parts 1* and *2* and *Hamlet*; for Geoffrey Wright, *Romper Stomper* and *Metal Skin*; for Jan Chapman Productions, *Naked: Stories of Men* and *Love Serenade*.

BRADLEY BYQUAR
ACTOR

Bradley graduated from Queensland University of Technology Academy of the Arts in 1989. His theatre credits include: *The Larrikin and the Bard, Shakespeare's Word* and *The Last of the Lands* (Grin and Tonic Theatre), *A Midsummer Night's Dream* (La Boite Theatre), *Through Murri Eyes* (Street Arts, Brisbane), *Capricornia* (State Theatre Company of SA, MTC and Queensland Performing Arts Trust), *The Dreamers* (Kooemba Jdarra), *The Singing Land* (Toe Truck Theatre), *Moorli and the Leprechaun* (Q Theatre), *Learning to Swim* (Entr'acte Theatre) and *Skin, The Loaded Ute* and *Antony and Cleopatra* (Australian People's Theatre, STC). In 1994 Bradley received a nomination for Best Actor in a Television Series for his performance in *Heartland*. Other television credits include *GP, Corelli, Police Rescue*, the *Blackout* series, *Dolphin Cove, Bony* and the documentary, *Frontier*.

Grant Street Traffic Closure

To enable work to begin on the Melbourne City Link project, Grant Street will be closed to all traffic between St Kilda Road and Sturt Street from April 1996.

Transfield-Obayashi, the joint venture contracted by Transurban to design and construct the project, requires access to Grant Street for the construction of two tunnels under the Domain and Yarra River to link the West Gate Freeway and the South-Eastern Arterial. Pedestrian access will be maintained alongside the Victorian College of the Arts and will be lit at night.

Grant Street will be closed to traffic until the tunnels are scheduled to open by the year 2000. Grant Street at Dodds Street will be redesigned at the completion of construction as a pedestrian precinct with its design reflecting the surrounding Arts Precinct.

Playbox will advise patrons of further developments as news comes to hand.

LILLIAN CROMBIE
ACTOR

Lillian studied classical ballet, jazz, modern and traditional dances with the Aboriginal and Islander Dance Theatre and with the Alvin Ailey American Dance Theatre before studying drama, voice and movement at NIDA and later with Redfern's Eora Centre. Theatre credits include Toe Truck Theatre's *Mereki, The Peacemaker* and *The Keepers* for the Aboriginal National Theatre Trust; Gunna Productions' *Between a Rock and a Hard Place;* Canberra Theatre Trust's *The Custodian, Gunjies* and the Nibago Production of *Black Mary*. Film and television credits include *Last Wave, A Place at the Coast, Deadly, Ring of Scorpio, Dolphin Cove*, the *Blackout* series, SBS Television's *ICAM The Master* series, ABC's *Heartland* and the documentary *Sunrise Awakening*. Other credits include the Queensland Performing Arts Centre production of *Boisterous Oysters; Akwanso, Fly South* and *D Week* for Griffin Theatre.

WAYNE FREER
MUSIC

Wayne has been working as a performer, composer and musical director in Australia and overseas for the past 15 years. A Bachelor of Music graduate from Adelaide's Elder Conservatorium, Wayne currently leads three bands and has recorded and performed throughout Australia with *Paul Kelly and the Messengers, Robyn Archer, The Mambologists, Adelaide Symphony Orchestra, Monica and the Moochers, Castanet Club, Speedboat, Jacky Orczascky and the Godmothers, Utungun Percussion, Toni Nation* and *David Addes*. His theatre work includes productions with Queensland Theatre Company, State Theatre Company of South Australia, Desoxy, Etcetera and in Company B Belvoir's production of *Aristophone's Frogs*. Wayne has also worked with 11 Australian Festivals, the 1991 Edinburgh Festival, the 1990 Singapore Fringe Festival, in Jakarta and the UK and with the 1993 Monte Carlo Olympic Bid.

GOOD HEALTHY BUSH TUCKER!!

When people over the years, examined the nature of traditional Koorie foods, the methods of cooking and preparation, as well as the balance of food used, it was and is clearly shown, that their traditional diets are as good as, or perhaps even better, than many modern western diets.

Food usage was, logically, related to seasons and locality. Generally, people ate an extremely wide variety of foods, including reptiles, fish, birds, mammals and vegetation.

Traditionally, Koories engaged in much physical activity due to the need to run and walk many kilometres to obtain food as hunter-gatherers. They were, unfortunately later prevented from practising this part of their culture, by the arrival of European settlers in Australia. These settlers supplied the Koories with flour, sugar, tea and small amounts of beef as their basic food, and having already been prevented from their normal practice of physical activity coupled with this new unbalanced diet, the first signs of disease and increased morbidity occurred.

The traditional Koorie diet was very rich in fibre and low in saturated fat, sugar, salt, and without alcohol. In certain areas of Australia where the diet of Aboriginal people is still largely unchanged, nutritional studies show that those bush foods eaten, have a very similar organic composition to corresponding cultivated healthy foods. So, we can learn something from our traditional Koorie healthy lifestyle, and should remember that brisk exercise, a healthy diet and a healthy lifestyle will assist with weight control, and may prevent not only diabetes, but also heart disease, high blood pressure and stroke.

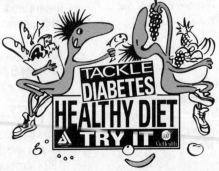

TACKLE DIABETES HEALTHY DIET TRY IT VicHealth

For further information regarding diabetes or a healthy diet, please telephone Diabetes Australia – Victoria on (03) 9654 8777

MARGARET HARVEY
ACTOR

Margaret graduated with a Bachelor of Arts in Drama from the Queensland University of Technology, Academy of the Arts, in 1993. Her television appearances include *GP* as well as the upcoming ABC series *Fallen Angels.* Her theatre credits include *Black Mary, The Dreamers,* (Kooemba Jdarra Performing Arts), *Somewhere in the Darkness* (Australian People's Theatre) and *Changing Time* (Salamanca Theatre Company, Tasmania). At QUT Margaret played Celia in *As You Like It* and Clytemnestra in *Agamemnon* and has also worked as an actor at the past three annual Australian National Playwrights' Conferences. She was also in *Wreckage* for ABC Radio and is a member of the band *Tamin*.

MARK HOWETT
LIGHTING DESIGNER

Mark began his career with Perth's National Theatre Company at the Playhouse in 1980. During that time he toured the US and UK, studying lighting design at Yale University with the aid of a Western Australian Arts Council Grant. He has designed lighting for numerous Australian and overseas theatre and opera companies, including the Australian Opera, Queensland Theatre Company, West Australia Opera Company, the Aboriginal and Islander Dance Theatre (Hong Kong tour), Danceworks (London tour), One Extra Company (Hong Kong and Jakarta tours) and the Auckland Opera – *The Flying Dutchman*. Productions he remembers with affection include *Jonah Jones* and *Crow* for the State Theatre Company of South Australia, *Sixteen Words for Water* and *Raindancers* for the Sydney Theatre Company, *Miss Bosnia, Corrugation Road* and *Bidenjarreb Pinjarra* for the Pinjarra Project.

GEOFF KELSO
ACTOR

Geoff, a NIDA graduate, appeared in *Royal Commission into the Australian Economy*, *Dead Heart* and *Bidenjarreb Pinjarra* at the 1996 Nambundah Festival for Belvoir St Theatre. He has also appeared in *Paddy* (Deckchair Theatre), *The Recruiting Officer* and *Our Country's Good* (Hole in the Wall), *Twelfth Night*, *Waiting for Godot* and *The Floating World* (Black Swan Theatre Co), *Brilliant Lies* (Perth Theatre Co), *Antony and Cleopatra*, *The Country Wife* and *Model Citizen* (State Theatre Company of WA) and *Die Fledermaus* (WA Opera and Opera Australia). Geoff also co-created *Bindenjarreb Pinjarra* (a play about the first recorded massacre of Aboriginal people in WA). In 1991, Geoff won the Swan Gold Award for Best Male Actor in WA for his performance in *Our Country's Good*, *The Recruiting Officer* and *Twelfth Night*.

JOHN MOORE
ACTOR

John started his career at the age of 14, in his grandfather Jack Davis' play *The Dreamers* at the 1980 Festival at Perth which then toured to the Portsmouth Festival in the UK. His theatre credits include *No Sugar* (1982 and again for Neil Armfield's production in 1989) and the national tour of *The First Born* (the award winning Jack Davis trilogy), the lead role in *Bran Nue Dae* and *Looking for the Southern Edge* (Black Swan Theatre Company). His film and television credits include lead roles in *Blackfellas*, *Deadly*, the telemovie *Heat*, *Bush Patrol* and most recently, the ABC-TV series *Fallen Angels*.

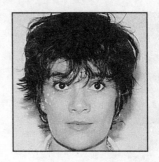

JILLI ROMANIS
ASSISTANT DIRECTOR
ASSISTANT STAGE MANAGER

Jilli is from the south-west coast of Victoria. She has worked for Theatreworks on *Titus*, *The Song of Songs* and *The Last Supper*. She then worked on the Black Swan Theatre Company's *Dead Heart* (directed by Neil Armfield), *Alleycat Alice and Friends, Sistergirl* and *The Floating World*. She is a graduate of the Aboriginal Performing Arts Centre Musical Theatre Course and in 1996 was a directing student at the West Australian Academy of Performing Arts where she assisted on *Dancing at Lughnasa* and *The Winter's Tale*. Jilli attended Amsterdam's International Theatre School and was Assistant Stage Manager and performer in Noel Tovey's *The Aboriginal Protesters* at the Weimer and Munich Festivals in Germany. Most recently she was involved with Black Swan Theatre Company's production of *Corrugation Road*.

FRANCESCA SMITH
DRAMATURG

Francesca is a director, writer, dramaturg and graduate of the 1994 NIDA Directors' Course. She directed John Patrick Shanley's *Danny and the Deep Blue Sea* for her graduation play and successfully restaged and produced it at The Stables Theatre in March 1995. She spent a year as Co-director of Playworks (National Women Writers for Performance Workshop) in 1995. She was Assistant Director on Cocteau's *Les Parents Terribles* for the Sydney Theatre Company and recently co-directed the Hot Young Things Festival of Young Writers for Australian Theatre for Young People. She recently assisted on the STC production of *Comedy of Errors* and is currently Dramaturg in Residence with Company B Belvoir.

BRIAN THOMSON
SET DESIGNER

Brian has designed many musicals,
movies, clips and numerous
productions for the STC, MTC, QTC,
STCSA, AO, VSO, AFI, on Broadway
and at Belvoir St Theatre for which
he has won a lot of awards.

IRMA WOODS
ACTOR

Irma is originally from Albany in
Western Australia. In 1994 she
studied at the Aboriginal Music
Theatre Program for six months and
1995 saw her study at the Western
Australian Academy of Performing
Arts as well as performing in the
production of *Capricornia*. In 1996
Irma was a student at the Aboriginal
Centre of Performing Arts and
involved in productions outside of
her studies. *Up the Road* is her
professional debut.

COMPANY Ⓑ

The originality and energy of Company B productions arose out of the unique action taken to save the Nimrod Theatre building from demolition in 1984. Rather than lose a performance space in inner city Sydney, more than 600 arts, entertainment and media professionals as well as avid theatre-goers formed a syndicate to buy the building. The successful syndicate included Robyn Archer, Neil Armfield, Gillian Armstrong, Peter Carey, Ruth Cracknell, Judy Davis, Mel Gibson, Max Gillies, Dorothy Hewett, Nicole Kidman, Sam Neil, Dame Joan Sutherland, Patrick White and David Williamson.

Belvoir St Theatre Limited is the owner of Belvoir St Theatre and the leasee of Wilson St Theatre. Company B is the resident production company operating under the artistic directorship of Neil Armfield.

THE BELVOIR ST THEATRE FOUNDATION Foundation Chair, Robert Crossman. Established to support the aims of Company B and to provide a solid financial base for the continuing evolution of the work of the Company B Actors.

COMPANY B BOARD Sue Hill, Alan John, Rachel Maza, Keith Robinson, Leigh Small, Brian Thomson and Barbara Tiernan (Chair).

BELVOIR ST THEATRE BOARD Maureen Barron, Hugh Barry, Tim Game, Wendy Harmer, Richard Harper, Deborah Kennedy, Yvonne Kux and Barry Otto.

WILSON ST BOARD Neil Armfield, Tim Burroughs, Yvonne Kux, Stuart McCreery, Tim McKenzie, Leisa Shelton and Kim Williams.

A special thank you for generous support: Ampol - production sponsor; Baker & McKenzie - looking after the legal needs of Belvoir St Theatre; Olivetti - provider of sophisticated computer equipment; Rothschild Australia - development workshop sponsor; Spicers Paper - supplier of very nice paper and the Sydney Morning Herald.

Company B Limited gratefully acknowledges the assistance of ATSIC, Aboriginal and Torres Strait Islander Arts Board, Literature Board and Performing Arts Board of The Australia Council, Opera Australia, Bray's Books Balmain, Burwood Press, CocaCola Amatil, Robert Crossman, Deloitte Touche Tohmatsu, Dendy Films, Desire Brand Management, EMAIL, Ffotograff, Roger Hind, Hoover Australia Information Tools, John Adams Hairdressing, NSW Ministry for the Arts, Red Star Cafe, South Sydney Council, Sydney Theatre Company, Penny Ward, Willflowers and Yann, Campbell, Hoare, Wheeler.

Australia Council

This project has been made possible with assistance from the New South Wales Government through the Ministry for the Arts

THE 🏛️ MALTHOUSE

PLAYBOX THEATRE CENTRE OF MONASH UNIVERSITY

When you've got the tradition, the pride and the spirit it shows in everything you do

Carlton. One of the world's great brewers.
CUB proudly supporting Playbox Theatre Company.

APB14902/A CN374

IAN: The Kooris in my department have got teams going. They're pretty good too. Guys play as well.

SUSAN: Mmm.

IAN: Yeah. I remember how good you were, Sue. Used to love seeing you play, your long black hair flying everywhere, and that gold sash flying up and down the court, your grunting everytime you threw the ball. I used to tell everyone that big WA on the back of your uniform stood for, "Woman and an 'alf".

SUSAN: It's wing attack. It stands for wing attack *alright*? Now go and sit somewhere else. I don't want trips down memory lane while I'm coaching please. We wouldn't be playing today out of respect for Auntie Sissy, but it's the Semi Final, so don't sit here like it's a day out in the park pissing in my ear. I just want to win this game and go home, OK.

IAN: I'm sorry. Maybe I shouldn't have come. It's just I promised Liddy I'd see her. I thought it would be nice to spend some time with you.

SUSAN: Well I'm busy right now.

　　　[*Pause.*]

　　What did you come back here for? Is this a holiday for you? Is that what it is –

IAN: You think I want to be here?

SUSAN: – A nice break from the office. Ya come down here and drop your H's for a while, rub a bit of tar back on, then back to Canberra to tell everyone nothin's changed on the mish, and you're glad you don't live there anymore. Your Uncle's dead! Isn't that why you're here?

IAN: This is not the time or place for this kind of discussion.

SUSAN: Yeah, you can jump back into your pinstripe suit and sound like a bureaucrat when ever you want, can't you Ian? Get up there you girls!

IAN: I can't win. If I didn't come you'd call me a bastard and now I am here, you're callin' me a bastard to my face. You're not right, Susan. I didn't deliberate about being here, I'm just here, OK, warts and all, I'm here.

SUSAN: And we're so thankful for it. You're just here. Maybe that's your problem, Ian. Wait for people to tell you what to do, where to go, what to say, who you are, who you're gonna be. Come on you girls!

IAN: At least I'm having a fucken go.

SUSAN: Yeah. Well some of us choose to stay home.

IAN: You know as well as I do why I left.

SUSAN: It was supposed to be for a couple of months.

IAN: Is that all you think Nat was worth? A couple of months.

SUSAN: Don't dump your shit on me. You really think Nat would have wanted you to turn your back on Aunt Sissy and Uncle Kenny?

IAN: You make it sound simple.

SUSAN: You just don't understand do you?

IAN: I understand I cried for two years when I left here. I understand I drank like a fish, still do, and am probably an alcoholic. I understand I work very hard, probably as a distraction, and as a result they've made me a big shot in Canberra. Don't tell me my faults, OK, I live 'em.

SUSAN: What did you think we were left with? We didn't go anywhere.

IAN: Yeah, and what did you do instead? What did yous do about Nat?

SUSAN: We got on with our lives and we survived. No thanks to you or your bloody mates in Canberra.

IAN: Yeah, and you're as mad as hell, and you're not gonna take it any more. I get paid to listen to blackfellas moaning about how hard it is to survive. I meet ten Susan Lockerbees a month, so don't think I had to come all the way down here to get a lecture off another one sister girl!

SUSAN: You've never met another Susan Lockerbee, and you never will. You stereotype as much as gubs do but you can't see past that fat ego of yours Mr Admin. Officer Level Three, can ya?

IAN: Yes!

SUSAN: Don't you ever wonder why you're meetin' ten Susans a month all saying the same thing? Or do you listen to them so your boss doesn't have to? You, the buffer zone who can't give 'em any answers.

IAN: You haven't known me for ten years –

SUSAN: Thanks for reminding me.

IAN: – so don't fucken analyse my life for me alright. You've always been here, safe in the nest! I've been out there and it's fucken cold, Susan.

SUE: At least I didn't use my brother's death as an excuse for ending a relationship I never wanted in the first place.

IAN: I'm outta here. And I'm not coming back. [*Starts to exit.*]

SUSAN: Good.

IAN: Yeah.

SUSAN: Come on girls, don't let 'em in, don't let 'em in! Stay there, stay there. Don't let 'em in. I said STAY THERE!!!

[IAN *sings.*]

SONG: "BROTHER NAT"

He had no great dreams or delusions of grandeur,
he hid in his boots and his cowboy hat,
lairy shirts, soft chuckles and a lopsided grin,
brother Nat......... brother Nat.

Over the sunrise I'm burning, not learning,
I'm making fire but I'm throwing no light,
success is empty as the house that's got plenty,
but the only one in it's alone... tonight.

I've been the far side of lonesome for half my life,
'cos half of me lies on the hill,
part of me's angry and part of me's sad,
and all of me's missing him still.

You could have shown me where to go my brother.
You could have told me where it's at.
You know I would have been the man you could have been.
The man you should have been oh Nat.

Look where I'm walking now,
look how I'm talking,
who would have thought it would all come to this?

How could I hide my heart for this long,
when I'm the man who would have died...
... in your place.

I've been the far side of lonesome for half my life,
'cos half of me lies on the hill,
part of me's angry and part of me's sad,
and all of me's missing him still.

END OF ACT ONE

ACT TWO

SUSAN'S SONG

Is this the bane of a black girl's life,
healing wounds and stopping strife,
I walk dark caverns with no light,
but I don't have to walk alone.

Is this the bane of a woman's life,
seems my time is not my own,
I got to get some light into these caverns of darkness,
why do I feel guilt when I've got the chance to move?

I can't give what I can't find,
and you're trying to rob me blind,
painting pictures in my mind
that I thought I threw away,
but from the ground they come again,
they make me weak but I can't bend,
and just to glance at them again,
takes me back a thousand miles.

For nearly half my life,
my heart was stabbed with ice,
and a general love for all
was my cloak, it kept me warm,
then that love is turned to rage,
and the hurt begins to rise,
there's a man who I despise,
who is standing in my light.

You make your problems your excuse,
how dare you push the right to prove,
I know that what you did you did,
because of the need to feed the pain,
tell me where does that lead to,

but an empty soul attuned
to an ache that made you move,
anywhere but where you should,
anywhere but where you should,
if you wanted to you could,
it's too late now it's no good.

SCENE NINE

GREG *and* LIDDY *are in the car.*

GREG: You keep that form up going into next week, and you will eat
'em alive, Lid. You were easily in the top seven players in the
team today.

LIDDY: [*she punches his arm*] There are only seven players in the
team, smartarse. Anyway, I won this didn't I? Couldn't have
been *too* bad out there.
   [*She holds up trophy.*]

GREG: You dazzled them, absolutely dazzled 'em. That's the best
wing attack strategy I've ever seen. They didn't know whether
you were coming or going.

LIDDY: That was Sue's doin'. She can be real cunning when she
puts her mind to it. Great coach though, eh!

GREG: Best coach I've ever had the pleasure of knowing.

LIDDY: You know I'm thinking of going professional. I hear there's
a lot of money in netball. If you're good enough.

GREG: Yeah, which country is that in, Liddy? You want to make
good money, you should go back and get a good education. I
keep telling you of all the courses you could go and do. Got all
that information sent to you.

LIDDY: Oh lighten up, that's all I ever hear from you, how I'm so
smart, but I'm wasting my life away, coz I'm nearly twenty and I
haven't got a degree.

GREG: That's right.

LIDDY: I just put us in the grand final, and you wanna get depressing
and talk about my future.

GREG: Yeah, alright, alright, stay a Year Nine graduate.

LIDDY: It must be Uncle Kenny's funeral. Everybody's snapping, snarling or telling me to go somewhere or do something. An' you know why?

GREG: Why's that?

LIDDY: Coz no one's being straight out around here. Everyone's playing little games. I'm the only one playing a *real one*.
[*She holds up trophy.*]

GREG: You think so.

LIDDY: I know so. Hey, Susan really jarred Ian up during the game.

GREG: Really?

LIDDY: Shame. Yeah, people was watching them instead of us.

GREG: Was Ian there? I didn't see him at all.

LIDDY: He took off. After he said he'd come and watch me play and all.

GREG: Yeah. Susan seemed a bit out of sorts afterwards. What was it all about?

LIDDY: I dunno. Why don't you ask her?

GREG: She'll tell me if she wants me to know.

LIDDY: You sweet on her or what?

GREG: Oh… we're just really good friends…
[LIDDY *starts singing, as she looks out the window.*]

LIDDY: "My boyfriend's back, you better cut out in a hurry, Shey-la, Shey-la, my boyfriend's back, If you don't stop, you'll get a permanent vacation…"

GREG: Liddy, you're so subtle, why don't you take up nursing, you'd have a great bedside manner.

LIDDY: Well, remember what I said before about playing games? Doesn't do you any good, just corks you up. That's all it does, just corks you up till before you know it, you'll explode all over the windowscreen, and have a car accident and kill me as well.

GREG: So just what do you think should be done about it in that case?

LIDDY: How long have you known her for, Greg Hidcombe, four years? You and her are always working together, socialising together. Yous drive each other everywhere. Anyone would think yous were married.

GREG: Come on. We really enjoy each other's company, that's all.

LIDDY: Yeah, but what are you gonna do about it?

GREG: Nothing. None of your business, sticky beak.

LIDDY: It's great though. Who'd have thought there'd be a love triangle in Flat Creek?

GREG: Stranger things have happened.

LIDDY: Such as?

GREG: What about the time three bullocks drowned in the dam and all their names started with G?

LIDDY: What?

GREG: Nothin!

LIDDY: Alright don't listen to me, no one ever does. That's my problem. I'm a born leader, but no one ever listens to me.

GREG: [*peering out window*] Isn't that Charlie with the fishing rods?

LIDDY: Yeah, he must be coming back from his "special spot" that everyone knows about. Stop the car. Let's see how badly he needs a lift.

GREG: Don't be silly, Lid, I'm gonna pick him up.

LIDDY: No, just stop the car.

> [*They stop. She toots the horn.*]

Look at him. He didn't even think coming and watching the Tigers play was worth worrying about. He'd rather go fishing. Don't give the bastard a lift. Let him walk, the big hunter.

GREG: Charlie and Liddy. Flat Creek Romeo and Juliet.

LIDDY: Oh, shut up. Here he comes. Am I gonna take off, Charlie Cardiff, or am I gonna stay and let you catch up to me? OK, he's close enough. Now reverse. Now take off. Over to the left and we'll get him with the dust. Oh Greg!

GREG: Now who's playing games Tiger?

LIDDY: RAAARGH!

SCENE TEN

IAN *is packing his stuff.*

SISSY: Hello, darlin'. You're back early.

IAN: Yeah. I didn't stay till the end.

SISSY: Ah.

IAN: Aunt, I was just thinking if it's alright with you I might go down and get a room in town. I just don't think it was a good idea to stay on the mission.

SISSY: What are you talking about?

IAN: I just think you've got enough to worry about without me stepping off the plane. I reckon Uncle Kenny's thrown me right into the middle of it.

SISSY: Come here my boy and give me a big hug.

[*They hug.*]

Uncle Kenny would have been real proud of you. You know that, eh. He would've wanted you to stay here, my boy. Come and sit down.

[*Both sit.*]

Is it the mob around here that are making you crazy, son?

IAN: One minute I hate this place and the next minute I hate myself.

SISSY: Of course it'd be hard, my boy. You've been through a lot and you've been away a long time. There's a lot we haven't talked about.

[*Silence.*]

IAN: I still miss him.

SISSY: We all do, bub. A wasted life's missed the most they reckon.

IAN: Yeah. [*Nods.*]

SISSY: When you left, you were as wild as hell. We got you out of here so you wouldn't do something silly. You know that, don't you. It's not because we didn't love you or we didn't want you to be here. I just wouldn't have been able to cope if we lost both of you. Nat always said you were the smart one. That you were gonna get somewhere. And you did.

IAN: Auntie I don't know where I got.

SISSY: You come a long way in nine years, my boy. You remember that picture of you in the paper when they were announcing that big policy for what's its name about five years ago.

IAN: Oh you could hardly see me in it.

SISSY: Course you could. I could still see you and I'm as blind as a bat. Well I've still got that clipping somewhere there in the shoebox. Kenny he rang me up and told me to buy the paper. He spotted you while he was away shearing. He always knew what was goin' on.

IAN: He was away a lot, wasn't he, Auntie? Shearing and things.

SISSY: I'm not gonna lie to you son, your Uncle Kenny was away more often than home, especially after you left. I missed him, but I adjusted, got used to not having him around. Women do, ya know.

IAN: You don't have to tell me, Aunt.

SISSY: It's no secret around here, don't be silly. Old bugger used to drop in for a gig more than anything else. You know to see if I was shacked up with some bloke or to check out the Co-op, stickin' his nose in. We had a falling out over that too. Never agreed. He had lots of good ideas but he wasn't around long enough to explain them.

IAN: I remember he made that toy sheep we could sit on, made it out of real fleece too. Me and Nat used to fight over it. We used to fight over everything.

SISSY: You two boys used to love outdoing each other. Nat just wanted to break in horses when he grew up. He would have laughed at you in your flash Canberra suit and that pirate earring.

IAN: Yeah, Nat Sampson, the Koori cowboy. Used to tell everyone he was the best rider in the district. I remember you bought him those boots for his birthday, just before he died. They were nice, embroidered stitching, steel toe. He used to be taller than me when he wore them. Then he got buried in them. What a waste.

SISSY: Uncle Kenny's going to be right next to Nat, my boy. It's beautiful up there. We keep it clean and weed it. He knows you're here you know, Nat I mean. Why don't you go up and say hello. Here I'll pick you some flowers for him.

IAN: Don't you want me to come to the luncheon, Aunt?

SISSY: Come a bit later, son. They're not going anywhere. I'm just having a breather before I go up. Ted an' Lucy'll be there. You remember 'em, son?

IAN: Yeah, Lucy with the false leg.

SISSY: Yeah. Must be hard for 'er, eh?

IAN: I remember when they stopped over on their way to the rodeo that time. I was just a little tacker. But it's hard to forget a

36

woman taking off her false leg and floggin' her man with it for losing their money in a two up game!

SISSY: And when he came to our house with his ear bleedin' and a split lip he said he'd never seen Lucy so hoppin' mad!

[*They both laugh.*]

IAN: Come on Auntie, I'll walk you to the hall first.

SISSY: I'll be right. I been up that road before. I been up that road.

SCENE ELEVEN

CHARLIE *and* LIDDY *enter the loungeroom.* LIDDY *still has her uniform on and is carrying her trophy.* CHARLIE *has a bucket.*

CHARLIE: Thanks for the lift, Greg. Maybe next time you can hit every pot-hole in the road, I'm sure we missed a couple back there. Look at this. Scales all over me, fuck me dead.

LIDDY: Don't swear. [*Yelling.*] Auntie, ya home?

[*Pause.*]

It's OK, ya can swear now. Anyway you shouldn't put so much water in the bucket, you'll drown the fucken things.

CHARLIE: Fish don't drown, you dupp.

LIDDY: They look dead to me, look at 'em, laying on their side.

CHARLIE: They were dead before I put 'em in the fucken bucket.

LIDDY: Well, why did you put so much fucken water in then big shot? They ain't gonna get any bigger.

CHARLIE: To keep 'em fresh.

LIDDY: There's only two of 'em. I think they'll fit in the fridge, Charlie.

CHARLIE: Y'know, when I was doin' Grade Twelve there was a girl just like you in my class. Her name was Hayley. And she was just like that Hayley's Comet too. Talked real fast, and went round and round in circles.

LIDDY: You should've held onto her, she might have taken you somewhere.

CHARLIE: No, I got bigger fish to fry.

LIDDY: I hope you don't mean them. Time they're cooked, you could spread 'em on a slice of bread.

CHARLIE: Yeah I bet you'll be right there when they're cooked too.

LIDDY: Sick of talking about them fish. I just got best on the court for the semi final. Let's talk about that. Even better let's drink about that, there's beer in the fridge, let's have a toast, eh!

CHARLIE: I'll be in that. I'll get 'em.

LIDDY: Hey why don't you get 'em?

CHARLIE: I'll just get the beer then will I.

[*Both laugh.* CHARLIE *goes to fridge.*]

LIDDY: Grab the bottom ones, they'll be colder.

[CHARLIE *gives her a beer.*]

CHARLIE: There you go, globe-trotter.

LIDDY: Speaking of which… [*Raises can.*]… here's to the Tigers, best team in the district!

CHARLIE: Ever wonder why gubs are always using animals from other countries as their emblem? Either that or weapons of destruction.

LIDDY: Such as?

CHARLIE: Bullets, bombers, cyclones, tornadoes, warriors, tigers, lions, broncos, bears…

LIDDY: Yeah. Wallabies, roos, swans, butterflies…

CHARLIE: Butterflies?

LIDDY: Anyway, I'm part of the Tigers so watch it.

CHARLIE: Oh yeah, well how come the rest of the team's still celebrating at their club, and you're sitting here with me?

LIDDY: I had to come back for Uncle Kenny's luncheon. You wouldn't understand that tho' would you, Moby Dick?!

CHARLIE: It's none of my business. To Uncle Kenny [*Raises can.*]

LIDDY: You're not funny Charlie, so quit while you're behind.

CHARLIE: I was born behind. Behind the fucking eight ball.

LIDDY: Oh, bring in the violins.

CHARLIE: Nah, I've gotta get out of here, Liddy. Head for the coast. Get a job.

LIDDY: Well there's plenty of jobs round here y'know. It's just that you don't always get paid for them. Look at me, I'm a born leader and I'm flat broke.

CHARLIE: Ah, but we'd follow you to the ends of the earth, Liddy Peters.

LIDDY: Nah, make me paranoid!

CHARLIE: Well, I'd follow you out of Flat Creek, anyway. I'm sick of this mob... no, I'm not. I'm sick of looking at Greg Skidmark's ugly fucken head. I'm sick of watching them prop up gubs while we stagnate.

LIDDY: You're always complaining about him an' the Council. Why don't you do something about it? When they had the Directors AGM, you went fishing again, didn't you, Charlie?

CHARLIE: Huntin'. I don't want nothing to do with 'em. Bunch of black sheep. Fucken Council.

LIDDY: Soon as you're eighteen you're old enough to be nominated. I would've nominated you. Everyone knows you're a Year Twelve graduate. You probably would've got in. But na, go fishin' and let the old women do all the work for you. Put 'em in their grave, then moan about them at the wake.

CHARLIE: You know you've been hanging around Susan too long. You're starting to sound like her, ya know that.

LIDDY: Thank you. That's a compliment I reckon. Na! I dream about going somewhere all the time. But I think I'd get homesick, be away too long.

CHARLIE: Don't you know anywhere in Australia's only a day's travel from here?

LIDDY: How, a day's travel?

CHARLIE: On a plane, that's how. Only cost you a few hundred dollars.

LIDDY: A few hundred. I haven't even got cab fare into town. Friggin' aeroplanes.

CHARLIE: Hey, Uncle Kenny used to say to me air hostesses are just waitresses without a cigarette in their mouths.

LIDDY: You're really mad, Charlie Cardiff, and you're getting madder all the time. Soon you'll be mad enough to want to stay.

CHARLIE: Of course, if I was made an offer I couldn't refuse...

[LIDDY *pours some beer in her trophy.*]

To us mind travellers, eh!

[*They toast.*]

To us, Liddy.

[*They kiss.*]
Liddy, you gotta go to that luncheon, you know.
LIDDY: It's just up the road.
   [*They kiss again at length.*]

SCENE TWELVE

IAN *is at Nat's graveside.*

IAN: Hey, brother, how do I look? Or have you been watching me for a while. I never got to tell you about the places I've been or the people I've met. I've travelled a bit. Went to Coober Pedy, had a go at mining. First day on the job I fell down a shaft and broke my arm. Decided mining wasn't for me. Some way or another I ended up in Canberra.

   You used to brylcreem my hair for me. I used to love the way you'd grab my ears like motor cycle handles and twist them? Vroom vroom. And that toy sheep we used to fight over. I was just talking with Auntie about it. Had a bit of a blue with Susie. She's been at my throat since I got back. They've all been having a go at me. They reckon it's easy. But they've never been off the bloody mission. They reckon I'm a coconut. She's a fiery woman.

   It's bloody fresh up here isn't it? Those boots of yours keep you warm? I got a big electric heater at home. I bought my own place now. What a whitefella, eh? A real house. Double brick. And I'm the only one in it. Well, you got the family up here. What've I got? I hate being alone. You all keep leaving me alone. Mum, dad, you. Now Uncle Kenny's gonna be up here. Yous'll be fucking right.

   What the fuck's going on? They're punishing me. Are you punishing me too? I didn't want to leave, Nat. They all told me to go. They made me go away. Not do nothing. I fucking hated 'em. They did jack shit. Those cops killed you and they did jack shit. Are you ashamed of me for that, my brother? If it was me they'd killed, you would've rode your horse into the fucken station and torn those cunts apart. That's what I wanted to do. But they made me go away. I thought you were a king and they

40

killed you like a fucken dog. I'm sorry, Nat, I'm sorry. You knew
I'd be back. You knew I'd be back here with you.

It's fresh, eh? I love you, Nat. I love you, brother.

HYMN: "AMAZING GRACE"

Amazing Grace how sweet the sound,
that saved a wretch like me.
I once was lost but now I'm found,
was blind but now I see.

Through many dangers, toils and snares,
I have already come.
Was Grace that brought me safe this far,
and Grace will lead me home.

Yet when this flesh and heart shall fail
and mortal life shall cease,
I shall possess within the veil,
a life of joy and peace.

Amazing Grace how sweet the sound,
that saved a wretch like me.
I once was lost but now I'm found,
was blind but now I see.

SCENE THIRTEEEN

The community hall, after the funeral. IAN *approaches* SUSAN.

SUE: I'm sorry about Uncle Kenny.

IAN: I'm sorry about everything. I really miss him today.

SUE: I feel like he's right here.

IAN: We uh…

SUE: What…?

IAN: Doesn't matter. Really.

SUSAN: Uncle Kenny came back playing the gum leaf a couple of
      years ago. Just taught himself. He played "The Road to
      Gundagai" like it was a saxophone.

IAN: Old bugger. He was always picking up something.

SUSAN: You're never too old to learn.

IAN: Guess not. Would you like a drink?

SUSAN: Yeah, that'd be good.

[IAN *goes to get a drink.* AUNT SISSY *enters with* LIDDY.]

There you are. I was wondering where you'd got to.

LIDDY: We were just saying a private goodbye to Uncle Kenny. Never seen so many flowers.

SUSAN: You right, Aunt? Can I get you a cuppa?

SISSY: Oh yeah. I'm dry as a tomcat's tit. It was a beautiful service, wasn't it?

SUSAN: It was perfect.

SISSY: He'd be happy. Smiling. He finally finished something, eh.

[LIDDY *gives* SISSY *a cup of tea.*]

Thanks love. You know, when he was away I could see him sometimes, in my mind. Half way up an orange tree or taking a drink outside a shearers' hut. He used to turn and smile right at me. That's what kept us going. You know, Kenny used to call us hindred spirits. For thirty-four years I never had the heart to tell him he meant kindred! [*Giggles.*] Or did he, eh?

[GREG *and* CHARLIE *enter with a bundle of cards.*]

GREG: How are you bearing up, Aunt Sissy? We collected these for you off the flowers.

CHARLIE: Yeah. We thought you might like to keep them.

SISSY: Thanks boys. They'll go in the shoebox. Aren't people lovely. Listen to this one. "Over the sunrise he'll be waiting for you. All our love, Lois, Kevin and the kids."

GREG: I'm sure he's going to be very sorely missed, Aunt Sissy.

SISSY: Yeah. I'm going to be missing you too, apparently, Greg. When are you finishing up?

GREG: Oh, in a couple of months, probably. Who told you?

SISSY: Oh you know what the Koori grapevine's like.

GREG: Yeah, Charlie Cardiff. The Flat Creek Kojak.

CHARLIE: Eh?

GREG: I'm going to miss this place. I'm sorry, Aunt Sissy. I was waiting for the right time to tell you myself.

SISSY: Mmm. Well, we're gonna have to find somebody good to fill your shoes.

GREG: Actually I've got some thoughts on that which we could talk about at a more appropriate time…

SISSY: No time like the present.

GREG: Well, funnily enough, there's someone right under our noses who's shown more than a passing interest in taking the position.

SISSY: Who?

GREG: Charlie Cardiff.

SISSY: Charlie Cardiff. [*She laughs.*] He's hardly set foot in the office.

GREG: Oh, I wouldn't say that. He knows the ins and outs of the office better than you think. He's got a lot of potential.

SISSY: Ain't that a turn up for the books.

LIDDY: Charlie would be fantastic, Aunt. He's a good hunter.

SISSY: That's gonna be a fat lot of use.

LIDDY: Yeah, well, you know what I mean…

SISSY: I thought you'd be putting in a bid for the job before Charlie, darlin'.

LIDDY: Oh, he's asked me to marry him, Aunt. So I'd be running the office anyway.

SISSY: What? What?

LIDDY: I know you have to advertise and all that but at least give him a chance. He'll probably leave if you don't. Then I'd have to go as well.

SISSY: Now just hold it right there. Who's gonna marry who?

LIDDY: I was born for Charlie Cardiff, Auntie. And Charlie Cardiff was born for me.

ALL: Oohh.

SISSY: Who spiked the punch? You and Charlie, eh? I always had a feeling about you two. I suppose no one could put up with you two except each other.

GREG: Well congratulations, Liddy. What a big day, eh?

SUSAN: Good on you Charlie. I reckon Uncle Kenny's real proud of you. He always wanted a blackfella lookin' after this place, eh Auntie.

SISSY: Ian, maybe you could train Charlie up a bit.

GREG: Mmm.

SISSY: After you've gone, Greg, I mean. You'll need to learn how to write submissions, fill out applications, handle the accounts, and work the computer.

IAN: Well, yeah, I could certainly help out from time to time. Wouldn't want to cramp his style though.

LIDDY: That's alright. Charlie Cardiff hasn't got any style.

CHARLIE: Oh gawd, we're sounding like a married couple already.

SISSY: Well in that case, Charlie can start next week with Greg. As long as it's OK with the Council, that is. But you're gonna have to behave yourself alright?

CHARLIE: No worries, Aunt.

IAN: He'll be right. I promise I'll keep an eye on him.

GREG: Me too.

SISSY: Yeah well, it takes a warrior to train a warrior.

GREG: Thanks, Auntie. I'll keep his nose to the grindstone.

SISSY: Mind you, the way the government's going, we'll be lucky to hold onto our Land Council.

IAN: Yep. The stormclouds are gathering.

SISSY: It's gonna get worse before it gets better.

GREG: Oh, I doubt that, Aunt Sissy. There'd be a huge uproar if the government tried to stop funding organisations like ours. It'd be blatant racism.

CHARLIE: And far be it from this government to appear blatantly racist.

SUSAN: Big words for a little man.

LIDDY: He's not a little man anymore.

ALL: True!!!

SCENE FOURTEEN

It is the morning after the funeral. SUSAN *is at* AUNT SISSY'*s when* GREG *appears at the doorway with flowers.*

GREG: G'day Sue, can I come in? I just called by your place. You weren't there.

SUSAN: No. I was here.

GREG: Yeah. I thought I'd drop in and see how Aunt Sissy's bearing up.

SUSAN: Oh, she's still in bed.

44

GREG: Uh.

SUSAN: I don't think she wants to see anyone right now, Greg, but it's nice of you to bring her flowers. I'll put them in some water. They'll die in this heat.

GREG: Uh, thanks. It was a beautiful service yesterday, it really was.

SUSAN: Yeah, it was beautiful.

GREG: I was going to suggest at our next meeting that we buy Kenny a tombstone from the discretionary fund. See what they think. Sissy would be too embarrassed to ask. But I think it's the least we can do after all the work she's put in, she hasn't got much put away.

SUSAN: Greg, that's a lovely thought'n all that, but maybe we should leave it up to the Directors.

GREG: Yeah, well we'll toss it round the table then. Sue, I've got something to talk to you about. As you know, I've been unofficially offered a position with the Australian Institute of Aboriginal and Torres Strait Islander Studies as a Policy Development Officer. They said it was mine if I wanted it. All I had to do was put in an application, which I'm sending tomorrow.

SUSAN: Yes. Congratulations. With everything yesterday I didn't get the chance to say we're really going to miss you around here.

GREG: Thanks. I've been stewing over it, and I decided four years is long enough here. I've loved every minute of it, I've learnt so much about people. I feel like part of the family. I feel I should move on. I wanted to talk to you because I wanted to ask you something. I think you better sit down. I feel very strongly about you Susie Lockerbee, have for a long time. I know I'm really springing this on you but would you consider coming with me?

SUSAN: Coming with you?

GREG: Susan, will you marry me?

SUSAN: Jesus, Greg, I'm shocked. I... uh, don't know what to say. You and I have always been friends. I never thought that... like uh... Greg, I think that you better sit down. Look Greg, I'm flattered. Shocked but flattered and...

GREG: I'm not asking you to say yes straight away. I'm giving you eight weeks to think about it and come to a decision before I leave. I've got accommodation lined up with a friend. There's enough room for the three of us till we find something else.

SUSAN: Hold on, Greg.

GREG: I'll be on a good salary, to support us.

SUSAN: Hold on…

GREG: Of course you could get a job easily there too. I've watched Lutana grow up and I'd be honoured to be her father. There'd be good schools there and…

SUSAN: Greg, you're not letting me finish.

GREG: Oh, sorry.

SUSAN: Look I'm flattered. No one's wanted me in that way in a long time and it's nice to hear you say that, it really is. But I think I'm too used to my home to go off and do that. And I always thought we were friends, good friends.

GREG: We are. That's why I know we could work. Better to be friends first, know each other as well as we do.

SUSAN: Yes.

GREG: Anyway I'll leave it with you. I don't want an answer today. Remember, you've got eight weeks. Tell Aunt Sissy I'll see her later today.

SUSAN: Look Greg, really…

GREG: Nope, don't want to hear it. By the way, the flowers were for you.

[GREG *exits.*]

SUSAN: Shit.

[IAN *enters in his suit, ready to leave.*]

IAN: Oh, sorry. I didn't know you were here. I was going to leave you a note. I have to catch my plane today. I have to be back by tomorrow. I'm glad I came this weekend, it's been great to see everyone, including you. It's just a shame that we only seem to get together when there's a funeral.

SUSAN: There's the taxi.

IAN: I've said goodbye to Aunt Sissy. I told her I'll be back soon. I hope yous look after her while I'm gone. Thanks for everything Sue. [*Kisses her.*] Don't walk me out. Bye.

> [SUSAN *notices that* IAN *has left his diary. She grabs it and runs to the door.*]

SUSAN: Ian!!

> [*The car leaves. She reads the diary.*]

I wish you'd stop reading my diary... Delilah. I'll be back for it. Luv Sampson.

THE END

APPENDIX

In the original production an alternative ending was added.

SUSAN: You forgot your diary.

IAN: I forgot a lot of things.

SUSAN: Including me, eh?

IAN: I've done a lot of stupid things in the last ten years, but I never forgot about you.

SUSAN: I thought you were just trying to block out the memory of losing Nat, and blocked me out in the process. I'd almost come to accept that. I was almost ready to forgive you. Until you showed up. Then I realised I was hurt and really pissed off.

IAN: Hell hath no fury like a woman scorned, eh?

SUSAN: Yeah well double it if she's black, and triple it if she's from my clan. My clan. It's my strength and sometimes it feels like my curse.

IAN: Even earth mothers need a break, Delilah.

SUSAN: Oh yeah.

IAN: Why don't you come to Canberra with me and have a little holiday? I've got a spare room.

SUSAN: Good. Lutana likes her own room.
[*She kisses him.*]
Canberra, eh. But I'm always gonna have a bit of this place inside me. If you know that it doesn't matter where you are. Flat Creek. Jail cell. Even Canberra. You've got this place in you too. Haven't you?

IAN: I guess I must have. When people ask me what it's like to be attached to the land, to try and explain it, I can't. I start to and then I get stuck with my words. I really want them to know. It's important that they know. That's another thing I forgot.

SUE: You been forgetting for your own sake. To protect yourself.

48

IAN: Hey, did you really mean all that stuff you said at the netball game?

SUSAN: I might have got a bit carried away. But I meant what I said about you running back to your office at ATSIC.

IAN: Uncle Kenny used to say that Aboriginal Affairs would cave in on itself 'cause it had no soul where it counted.

SUE: Yeah, we gotta start remembering that we are Aboriginal Affairs.

IAN: What do you think's gonna happen?

SUE: Oh, we'll probably get married and have a whole swag of kids.

IAN: I meant about ATSIC,

SUE: Let's worry about that up the road.

THE END